BUILDING STRESS RESILIENCE

Self-coaching questions, inspiration, tips, and practical exercises for becoming an awesome manager

⌘

Managerial Competencies Series
Playbook No. 4

CÉLESTE GRIMARD

Copyright © 2018 Céleste Grimard, Canada

All rights reserved. All materials on these pages are copyrighted by Céleste Grimard. Reproduction, modification, storage of all or a part of this book in a retrieval system or retransmission, in any form or by any means, electronic, mechanical, or otherwise is strictly prohibited without prior written permission from the author. Although every effort has been made to indicate the sources of text and ideas, it's possible that we missed some! If you're aware of references or citations that haven't been provided, please be sure to contact the author. This book does not constitute legal advice and isn't a substitute for independent professional advice.

ISBN-13: 978-1979023375

CreateSpace, Charleston, SC USA

⌘
ACKNOWLEDGMENTS

I originally developed this series as a self-study, self-paced program for hundreds of managers working in a geographically dispersed area. Over the span of many years, these awesome managers offered me feedback, inspiration, and encouragement to transform this program into a series of practical, easy to read books accessible to all managers. Thank you! I also thank Rhiannon Ward for her assistance in editing and proofreading the books in this series.

CONTENTS

Series Introduction   1

Introduction   3

    1. Reality Check: Self-Coaching Questions   17

    2. Inspiring Your Journey   31

    3. Tips for Awesome Managers   40

    4. Dilemmas: What Would You Do?   62

    5. Planning For Action   71

About the Managerial Competencies Series   74

References   98

BUILDING STRESS RESILIENCE

Welcome to the Managerial Competencies Series!

The aim of this series is to help you understand and build the core competencies you need to become an awesome manager.

There's no getting around it. There are tons of journals, books, blogs, videos – you name it – on the topic of managing. Yes, a lot has been written and said about how to be an effective manager. Everyone has their own spin to put on this topic, and research studies on this topic are practically endless. How does a busy manager sort through all the fads and fashions to find the nuggets of wisdom?

In designing this series, I pored over loads of resources and talked with hundreds of managers. I set aside all the fashions, fads, and fantasies, and I extracted only what is likely to be of enduring value to you. Although this series is

BUILDING STRESS RESILIENCE

geared towards practical, immediate use, I hope that it will provoke you to think deeply about managing and your role as a manager, and that it will make a difference for you so you can make a difference for others.

This module – Building Stress Resilience – is the fourth of 15 books, each covering a key competency of awesome managers. **Turn to page 74 to learn more about this series**, including the full slate of books, how each book is structured, and tips on how to get the most out of them.

Throughout the book, I will refer to your **learning journal** and your **feedback team. These helpful tools are explained on pages 89 and 90.**

BUILDING STRESS RESILIENCE: INTRODUCTION

Awesome managers are resilient in the face of stress.

BUILDING STRESS RESILIENCE

We have all experienced stress, and we have all heard someone talk about their stressful day. Sometimes we use the word "stress" as a catch all phrase that means pressure, upsetting, distressful, or demanding. But what is stress? According to Hans Seyle, the pioneer of stress research, stress is "a non-specific response of the body to any demand made upon it." Stress is "nonspecifically induced" because, while very specific changes happen in the body, these changes can be the result of many different things (i.e., from a kiss to a car accident). The demand can be a threat, a challenge, or any kind of change that requires the body to adapt.

We usually associate stress with its negative aspects. The positive side is that stress can help us perform at an optimal level by giving us mental alertness, increased energy, improved memory and recall, sharper perceptions, higher motivation, and calmness under pressure. This is why stress is considered an essential element of life. What is important is that people identify a level of stress that is personally productive and healthy and then

BUILDING STRESS RESILIENCE

operate from this optimal level. It is a matter of learning to manage stress rather than letting stress manage you.

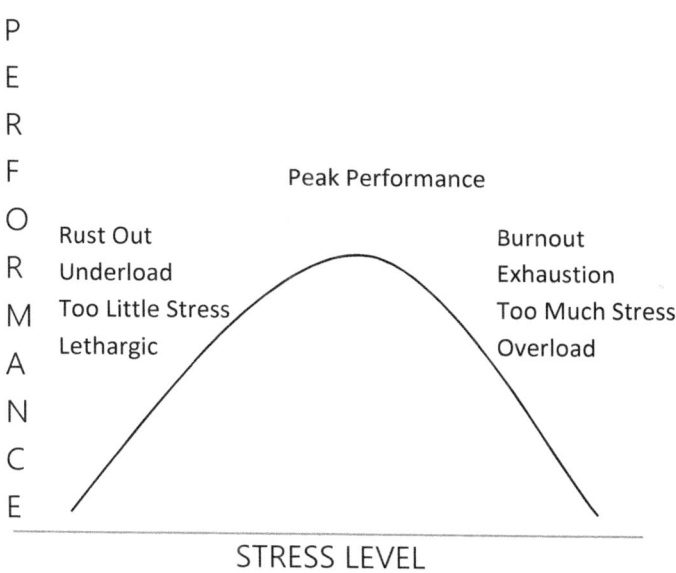

Work stress over a long period of time usually results in distress and, eventually, illness. In 1975, Dr. Herbert Freudenberger was the first person to coin the term "burnout." He defined it as "to deplete oneself, to exhaust one's physical and mental resources. To wear oneself out by excessively striving to reach some unrealistic expectation imposed by oneself or by the values of society." It is a condition that evolves over a period of prolonged stress and expenditure of energy. Burnout is a syndrome in which people feel emotionally exhausted and, as a result, begin to feel cynical about their work and depersonalize others (i.e., treating them as objects; for example, referring to a patient as "the kidney in room 212"). At the same time, people who are burnt out feel a reduced sense of personal accomplishment and efficacy (or effectiveness) on the job.

Is it lazy or carefree people who burn out? Nope! This is unlikely since, to be "burnt out" suggests that people were once "on fire" – strongly committed and devoting energy to their work. Indeed, Freudenberger's research suggests that people who suffer from burnout are "in a state of fatigue or frustration brought about by devotion to a cause, a way of life or a relationship that failed to produce the expected reward." Research also indicates that younger employees have higher burnout levels than older employees. However, it is possible that those who have remained in their profession for many years have found ways to adapt to the many demands of their roles.

Stress as a Management Concern

Stress is expensive for organizations. Work stress is associated with accidents, absenteeism, turnover, reduced productivity, in addition to increased health care costs to society. Based on their 2017 survey of thousands of workers, Mental Health America concluded that stress costs employers over $500 billion or more annually. In his review of survey results, Dan Cook found that 30% or more respondents were absent from work from 2 to 30 days each month due to stress at work. Often, organizations hope that stress will "go away" if they send folks to stress management workshops. Although such workshops may help employees deal with their

BUILDING STRESS RESILIENCE

reactions to stressful work conditions, the best solution is to deal with the stressful work situations (the sources of stress) directly.

The Stress Process

At its core, the stress process includes four elements – the **stressors** that cause **stress** which, in turn, result in a number of **symptoms**, and the **coping resources** that help to buffer or lessen the effects of stressors on stress. If you have lots of stressors but also have good coping resources, you will experience less stress and fewer negative health outcomes.

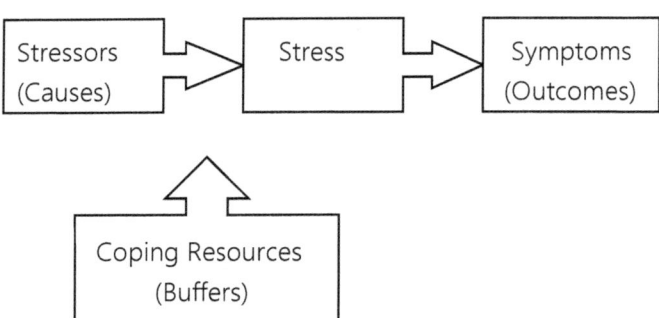

BUILDING STRESS RESILIENCE

Stressors (Causes)

The stress process begins with stressors. These are anything that causes feelings of strain or tension. There are many sources of stress in the workplace. Decades of research indicate that the most likely workplace stressors are (in order of importance): interpersonal conflict, perceived work overload, and role ambiguity (getting unclear messages about priorities). Additional predictors of stress include feeling a lack of control and/or participation in decision-making, and factors in the physical and psychological climate. People who feel a sense of control over their work, are involved in decision-making, and work in a safe environment (physically and psychologically) experience lower levels of stress.

Symptoms (Outcomes)

Symptoms are the results or outcomes of stress. They are often what people think about when they consider how "stressed" they are.

BUILDING STRESS RESILIENCE

Although many kinds of symptoms (physical, emotional, mental, spiritual, and relational) exist, most people find that they have a particular pattern of symptoms. Also, people with high levels of stress or burnout tend to have many symptoms. As the Canadian Centre for Occupational Health and Safety indicates in their table below, symptoms may gradually increase if not attended to at an early stage.

Stages of Stress
Phase 1: Warning (more emotional than physical signs, year or more before it's noticeable)
-Vague anxiety
-Depression
-Boredom
-Apathy
-Emotional fatigue
Phase 2: Mild Symptoms (intensified warning signs; after 6-18 months of continued stress; physical signs evident)
-Sleep disturbances
-Frequent headaches/colds
-Muscle aches
-Physical and emotional fatigue
-Withdrawal from others
-Irritability
-Intensified depression

BUILDING STRESS RESILIENCE

Phase 3: Entrenched Cumulative Stress (occurs when phases 1 & 2 are ignored; starts to have impact on career, family life and personal well-being)

-Increased use of alcohol, smoking, non-prescription drugs
-Depression
-Physical and emotional fatigue
-Ulcers
-Marital discord
-Intense anxiety
-Rigid thinking
-Withdrawal
-Restlessness, sleeplessness

Phase 4: Severe Cumulative Stress Reaction (self-destructive; occurs after 5-10 years of continued stress)

-Careers end prematurely
-Asthma
-Heart conditions
-Severe depression
-Lowered self-confidence
-Inability to perform job
-Inability to manage personal life
-Withdrawal
-Uncontrolled anger, grief, suicidal or homicidal thinking
-Muscle tremors
-Extreme chronic fatigue
-Agitation, over-reaction to minor events
-Frequent accidents
-Carelessness, forgetfulness

BUILDING STRESS RESILIENCE

Personal Coping Resources (Buffers)

Well-developed coping skills help people deal with stressors more effectively and, as a result, they feel lower levels of strain. Although they're important, coping skills tend to deal with the effects of stressors, and, as a result, are no substitute for directly addressing the causes of stress.

There are many ways to cope with stress. The first, and most important, is **personal care** through diet, exercise, sleep, relaxation, and other health habits. Personal care enhances a person's general resistance to experiencing stress. Another coping skill is seeking **social support** or the comfort and advice of others (as opposed to isolating yourself). Finally, an important coping skill that helps people deal with stress head on is **direct action,** or tackling the causes of stress through a problem-solving approach. It's the opposite of **escape coping** in which people ignore or avoid dealing with problems that might exist, perhaps hoping that they will simply go away on their own.

BUILDING STRESS RESILIENCE

In addition to these traditional resources, you can develop your hardiness and resistance to stress by building personal mastery and organizational competencies such as:

→ Taking responsibility for your actions and reactions.
→ Building emotional resilience.
→ Having a positive and optimistic attitude.
→ Demonstrating confidence in yourself.
→ Continuously improving your level of competence.
→ Putting a reasonable amount of effort and care into your work.
→ Being adaptable and flexible in response to changing demands.
→ Effectively organizing your time and space.

A Stress Metaphor

Now that you've seen a model of the overall stress process, let's use an analogy to get another perspective of it. Imagine that stressors are like a garden hose that is spraying water at various levels of pressure. If you're

BUILDING STRESS RESILIENCE

experiencing many stressors, then the water is spraying out at full volume and intensity. How you experience this onslaught of water (possibly through the expression on your face) represents the stress that you feel. An umbrella and rain gear represent your coping skills. By putting on rain gear and using an umbrella, you protect yourself from getting too wet (or strained). However, if the water from the garden hose comes at you at full pressure for an extended period of time, your rain gear might not be able to protect you, and you might get tired of holding the umbrella.

What would be the ideal response to this situation? Get a bigger and better umbrella or heavyweight rain gear that covers you from head to toe? These are good choices if there's absolutely no way that you could turn off the garden hose. However, the more direct and lasting approach is to turn off the garden hose or, at least, reduce the flow of water. You may need to ask the person who is holding the garden hose (in other words, someone who has some influence and control over the

BUILDING STRESS RESILIENCE

stressors) to lower the water pressure or turn it off completely. Thus, the most effective way to manage stress is to deal with its causes.

If the source of the water is rain, unless you can change the weather, stopping the rain would be impossible. Although it can be pleasant to walk in the rain at times (in other words, experience a moderate amount of stress), after a while, doing so becomes rather draining. In this case, wearing heavy rain gear or going inside a building (leaving the scene) might be the only actions that you can take to deal with the rain.

The building that you enter might represent a vacation or a break of some sort. Both vacations and breaks are effective in reducing stress levels in the short term. They provide much needed time away from stressors that can be used to put things in perspective. However, since they don't deal with the cause of stress, when you return from your time off (or "go back outside"), the conditions may be unchanged.

BUILDING STRESS RESILIENCE

The building might also represent your non-work involvements. For example, you might take refuge in the safety of your family. Work-family stress research has consistently found that employees tend to bring their stresses home with them and bring resources from home (support from family and friends; personal coping skills) to the workplace. Thus, the work-family boundary is asymmetrically permeable. This means that employees bring more "stuff" home with them than the reverse; this "stuff" consists of all the stressors and demands that people experience at work. Work-family balance programs can help in this regard but only if senior managers actively encourage their use.

1

REALITY CHECK: SELF-COACHING QUESTIONS

To help you examine your stress resilience skills and challenges, we invite you to ask yourself a series of self-coaching questions. Although most of these questions were developed specifically for this book, several were adapted from two great resources: *Structured Exercises*

BUILDING STRESS RESILIENCE

in Stress Management and *The Relaxation & Stress Reduction Workbook.*

While **thinking about your thoughts, feelings and behavior in the past six months** or so, find specific examples that support your answers. Consider whether or not "counter examples" exist; in other words, times when you may not have behaved in a manner that is consistent with your answer. Your answers to these self-coaching questions will help you assess your level of stress and your coping skills.

Take care to reflect honestly about these questions. While the Reality Checks in previous books have focused mainly on your *actions* at work, this one will require you to check in with yourself and be honest about your *thoughts, feelings, reactions, and behaviors* when it comes to stress. If you know yourself well, your answers will be right on the mark. Sometimes it's hard to analyze these things accurately if you're not used to assessing yourself or if you feel uncomfortable with the idea of reflecting on your own behaviors. But if you challenge yourself to be honest and approach these questions with an open mind, your answers will help shine a light on how you experience and cope with stress.

In all cases, but especially when your answers are extreme (in any direction), seeking candid and honest feedback from people you trust can be a valuable way of shedding light on your actual competency levels. In other words, you can learn a lot more about yourself if you get feedback from others.

You can ask people to answer some of the self-coaching questions for you and provide examples or anecdotes of situations that illustrate their answers. They may not tell you what you want to hear, but it may be exactly what you need to help you make progress on your journey toward becoming an awesome manager. As American writer Herbert Sebastian Aga said in his book *A Time for Greatness*, "the truth that makes men free is, for the most part, the truth which men prefer not to hear."

Asking others for feedback takes courage on everyone's part. Others don't necessarily have the same picture of you as you have of yourself, and people are sometimes reluctant to "tell it like it is." However, "feedback-lite" that is polite and tells you what you hope to hear won't help you grow as a person. Tell people that you need the straight goods.

Symptoms of Stress

Physical Symptoms
→ Am I having trouble sleeping at night?
→ Do I feel tired during the day?
→ Am I having more health problems (e.g. colds, indigestion, headaches) than usual?
→ Has my appetite changed?
→ Am I drinking more coffee or other caffeinated drinks, smoking more cigarettes, or using more alcohol or drugs?
→ Do I feel physically depleted?

Emotional Symptoms

→ Do I feel anxious, worried, or frustrated?
→ Am I moody, irritable, or impatient over small inconveniences?
→ Do I feel sad, ineffective, or depressed?
→ Do I feel very little enthusiasm or joy?
→ Am I feeling emotionally callous about the problems and needs of others?

Mental Symptoms

→ Am I forgetful?
→ Am I having difficulty concentrating?
→ Has my thinking been less clear than usual?
→ Has my decision-making been less effective than usual?
→ Do I tend to have a negative or pessimistic attitude about things?

Spiritual Symptoms

→ Have I lost a sense of meaning in life?
→ Does it feel like I've lost my sense of direction or purpose?
→ Do I feel like I don't really care about what happens anymore?

- → Do I feel spiritually depleted?
- → When I ask myself why I get up and go to work, is "my paycheck" the only answer I can come up with?

Relational Symptoms
- → Are my communications with others strained?
- → Do I feel isolated from others?
- → Do I feel like I can't trust others to have my best interests in mind?
- → Do I find myself complaining about or lashing out at others?
- → Do I tend to distance myself from others?

Evaluating Stress
- → Do I feel stressed out and used up?
- → Do I feel strained?
- → Do I feel like I'm at the end of my rope?
- → Do I feel exhausted?
- → On a scale of 1 to 10 (1=no stress, 10=extremely stressed), how stressed do I generally feel at work?

Sources of Stress

Lack of Control
→ Do I lack the authority needed to carry out my responsibilities?
→ Do I feel trapped in my situation without any real options for "escape"?
→ Do I feel that I have little control over what happens at work?
→ Do I feel that I can't solve the problems assigned to me (due to workplace policies and practices or a lack of skills)?

Information Gap
→ Are my job responsibilities unclear?
→ Do I lack the information needed to carry out certain tasks?
→ Do others not know what my responsibilities are and aren't?
→ Do I feel out of the loop about what's happening in my organization?
→ Am I unsure about the criteria used to evaluate my performance?

BUILDING STRESS RESILIENCE

Cause and Effect

→ Is the relationship between how I perform and how my performance is rated weak?
→ Is there very little relationship between how I perform and how I am treated?
→ Do popularity and politics seems to be more important than performance?
→ Am I unsure about what my manager thinks of my performance?
→ Am I confused about what I'm doing right and what I'm doing wrong?

Conflict

→ Am I expected to satisfy conflicting needs and demands?
→ Do I have disagreements or arguments with my coworkers? My manager? My clients?
→ Am I caught in the middle between people who are fighting with each other?
→ Do I tend to have negative interactions with others?
→ Do I feel bullied or intimidated by others?

BUILDING STRESS RESILIENCE

Blocked Career
→ Do I feel pessimistic about opportunities for advancement in my job?
→ Is my manager critical of me?
→ Is my good work going unnoticed?
→ Does my progress on the job seem slower than it should be?

Alienation
→ Do I feel alienated from others at work?
→ Do I feel unappreciated or unaccepted by the people I work with?
→ Do I feel unsupported by my coworkers and manager?
→ Do my values seem at odds with those of management?
→ Does the organization seem insensitive to my individuality?
→ Do I feel like I can't be myself at work?

BUILDING STRESS RESILIENCE

Overload
→ Do I have too much to do and too little time in which to do it?

→ Do I take on new responsibilities without letting go of any current ones?

→ Do I have to work on my own time (during breaks, lunch, at home, etc.) just to keep up?

→ Do I have so much work to do that I have trouble doing it well?

Underload
→ Do I have too little to do?

→ Do I feel overqualified for the work I usually do?

→ Is my work too easy? Routine? Boring?

Environment
→ Do I find my work environment to be unpleasant?

→ Do I lack the privacy I need to concentrate on my work?

→ Do some aspects of my work environment

seem hazardous?
- → Do I have lots of contact with unpleasant people?
- → Do I have to deal with many little hassles?

Conflict in Values
- → Am I required to do things or make decisions that are against my better judgment?
- → Do I have to make compromises in my values?
- → Do my family and friends express disrespect or apprehension about what I do?
- → Do I observe my coworkers doing things that I don't approve of?
- → Am I pressured to do things that are unethical or unsafe?

Lack of Participation
- → Am I unable to influence decisions that affect me?
- → Do decisions seem to be made in an arbitrary manner?
- → Do attempts at involving staff seem

superficial and/or inequitable?
- → Do my suggestions and ideas seem to be disregarded or undervalued?
- → Do I feel that I have little impact on what happens in my organization?

Coping with Stress

Personal Care
- → Do I eat a well-balanced, moderate, and healthy diet?
- → Do I get regular exercise?
- → Do I get enough sleep every night?
- → Do I know how to relax myself?
- → Do I avoid smoking and excessive drinking?
- → Do I see my doctor when needed?
- → Do I take regular breaks or vacations?

Social Support
- → Is there someone that I can talk to about almost anything?
- → Do I feel comfortable asking others for advice and support?

BUILDING STRESS RESILIENCE

- → Do I feel comfortable talking about my feelings and experiences with others?
- → Do I get the support I need from others?
- → Do I often get good ideas from others about how to solve a problem?
- → Do I feel that at least one person understands and cares about me?
- → Do I feel comfortable seeing a counsellor or another professional to talk through issues?

Direct Action

- → When I have a problem, do I try to deal with it head on?
- → When I feel stress, do I figure out what is causing it and try to address it?
- → Do I take initiative in resolving any difficulties that I might be experiencing?
- → Or, do I spend lots of time griping about a problem, but rarely try to fix things?

Reflection

What do your answers say about your perception of your stress level, the causes of your stress, and how you're coping with it? In the Symptoms, Evaluation, and Sources of Stress sections, the more "Yes" answers and examples you have, the more stress you're experiencing and the more you're feeling its impact. In the Coping section, more "Yes" answers and examples indicate a healthy approach to managing your stress.

These can be tough questions to reflect on. They may have brought up memories of challenging situations, moments you aren't proud of, or skills that you could improve. They may be unpleasant reminders of things in your work life that cause you strain. The important takeaway here is feeling motivated to work on improving your personal resilience to stress and your environment.

2

INSPIRING YOUR JOURNEY

As you read through the following quotations, take note of the ones that speak to you the most. Then consider the message they are conveying to you.

BUILDING STRESS RESILIENCE

Stress is the spice of life. - *Hans Selye*

⌘

What happens is not as important as how you react to what happens. - *Thaddeus Golas*

⌘

Those who think they have no time for bodily exercise will sooner or later have to find time for illness. - *Edward Stanley*

⌘

The human body is the best picture of the human soul. - *Ludwig Wittgenstein*

⌘

Take away the cause, and the effect ceases.

- *Miguel de Cervantes*

⌘

The mass of men lead lives of quiet desperation. - *Henry David Thoreau*

⌘

Regular exercise is one of the bet methods of relieving stress. - *Arthur Fisher*

BUILDING STRESS RESILIENCE

Do not anticipate trouble or worry about what may never happen. Keep in the sunlight.

- *Ben Franklin*

⌘

At times of great stress, it is especially necessary to achieve a complete freeing of the muscles. - *Constantin Stanislavski*

⌘

You've got to think about "big things" while you're doing small things, so that all the small things go in the right direction. - *Alvin Toffler*

⌘

Decide to focus on one thing at a time, instead of trying to solve everything at once. Just do that one thing, then you will feel a sudden decrease in stress. - *Gudjon Bergmann*

⌘

When one door closes, another opens; but often we look so long at the closed door that we do not see the one which has opened for us. - *Helen Keller*

BUILDING STRESS RESILIENCE

If the problem can be solved, why worry? If the problem cannot be solved, worrying will do you no good. -*Santideva*

⌘

If you don't like something, change it; if you can't change it, change the way you think about it. - *Mary Engelbreit*

⌘

Living one's life as if it is a competition between oneself and others is an inevitable path to a stressful life. - *Edmond Mbiaka*

⌘

Life is not a matter of having good cards, but of playing a poor hand well.
- *Robert Louis Stevenson*

⌘

When you find yourself stressed, ask yourself one question: Will this matter in 5 years from now? If yes, then do something about the situation. If no, then let it go.
- *Catherine Pulsifer*

BUILDING STRESS RESILIENCE

When you want to arrive at your goal more than you want to be doing what you're doing, you become stressed. - *Eckhart Tolle*

⌘

A crust eaten in peace is better than a banquet partaken in anxiety. - *Aesop*

⌘

For the sake of making a living, we forget to live. - *Margaret Fuller*

⌘

It's not the load that breaks you down; it's the way you carry it. - *Lou Holtz*

⌘

Stop focusing on how stressed you are, and focus on how blessed you are. - *Anonymous*

⌘

Stress is like spice. In the right proportion, it enhances the flavor of a dish; too little produces a bland, dull meal; too much may choke you. - *Donald Tubesing*

BUILDING STRESS RESILIENCE

You can see that our lives are, to a large extent, spent in avoiding confrontation with ourselves. And then you can begin to make sense of the enormous amount of culture's daily activities which attempt to distract us from ourselves, from a deep reflection, from deep thinking, from existential confrontation. There's a wonderful phrase by the philosopher Kierkegaard: "tranquillization by the trivial."

- Ray Walsh

⌘

Suppose a man gave you a car – free. He said, this is for you, and you can have it, for nothing. Imagine your delight. You ask if there's a catch, or a trick, or a snag. He says, no, not at all; this is for you, and you can have it: but there is just one thing to remember – you can never, ever have another one. Notice how your immediate reaction is, well, I must be very careful to look after this one. This story demonstrates exactly the position you are in with regard to your body. *- Paddy O'Brien*

BUILDING STRESS RESILIENCE

A Parable (*source unknown*)

Often when people are upset...
    or don't find much meaning...
    or damage a relationship...
    or are going too fast...
    or have lost something important...

Pretty soon they don't feel so good anymore...
    and they get sick.

So they go to the doctor...
    who looks at them...
    and fixes them...
    and gets them back on their feet...

And then, because they haven't learned why they got sick, some people...
    go home...
    and they get upset again...
    and damage a relationship...
    and still don't find much meaning...
    and go too fast again...
    or lose something important again.

BUILDING STRESS RESILIENCE

And in not too long...
    they don't feel good anymore...
    and they get sick again.

It's kind of wasteful and painful...
    but sometimes people go like this...
    getting up and down forever...
    That is until they get sick...
    and can't get gotten up again.

There are a lot of skills for dealing with
    being upset...
    not finding meaning...
    going too fast...
    damaged relationships...
    grief over losses...

There are plenty of skills for dealing with stress.

What about you?
    Is stress killing you?

What do you see in your life now?
    Stress Kills or Stress Skills?

BUILDING STRESS RESILIENCE

What are your five favorite quotations?

Why do these stand out for you?

Which would you want to adopt as your personal motto? Include on the signature line of your emails? Post on your desk?

# 3

TIPS FOR AWESOME MANAGERS

As you review the following list of actions for building stress resilience, circle, check, or highlight those that are especially meaningful for you. These tips come from a variety of sources including: Dr. Rita Nachen Gugel, Herbert Freudenberger, New Zealand Health Services, and Texas Women's University Counseling and Psychological Services.

BUILDING STRESS RESILIENCE

Direct Action

1. Be the "captain of your ship." If your job, your relationships, a situation, or a person is dragging you down, try to alter the circumstances, or if necessary, leave. If you aren't happy with your life, think about what's wrong or missing, and then plan the necessary actions to change it to match your needs and desires for your life. Don't drift along in difficult and stressful situations hoping that they will simply resolve themselves. They rarely do! Instead, change or end a bad situation.

2. Face up to your problems. Sort them out, and see which ones are real and which are simply imagined. Deal with them as they are, not what you think they are. Sometimes, when describing a problem to someone else, you realize that it's not such a big deal after all. When you put your problems in perspective, you may find that

some of them are simply not worth your time and effort.

3. Reduce the amount of "intensity" in your life. Pinpoint the most intense or stressful areas, and work toward relieving that pressure. This involves identifying stressors that are especially problematic for you and developing an action plan to address them. Deal with one problem at a time. Sort out your priorities, and deal with them in the order of their importance to you.

4. For an especially big stressor, do a force field analysis. Draw a vertical line down the center of a sheet of paper, labeling one side as (A) "Forces for change" and the other side as (B) "Forces preventing change." Identify: (A) what might persuade you to directly confront and address the stressor; and (B) what is stopping you from taking any action in this area. If the B column is longer and "stronger," then this might be why you're avoiding taking

BUILDING STRESS RESILIENCE

action. Kurt Lewin, the originator of force field analysis has found that, although most people focus on strengthening (A), the most effective way to create change is to reduce the barriers listed in column (B). Your task, then, is to review the entries in column (B) and address them.

5. Keep a record of all the hassles that you experience over a seven day period. Look for patterns and themes (i.e., some common problems). Try to eliminate as many hassles as you can.

6. Learn to say "No" to extra projects, social activities, and invitations for which you don't have the time or energy. This takes practice, self-respect, and a belief that everyone, needs quiet time to relax and be alone every day.

7. Try to put things in perspective. When you take everything personally, the weight of the world is on you. Don't make a

mountain out of every molehill that you come across. And, learn to delegate, not only at work but also at home and with friends.

8. Accept what you cannot change. Change what you can, if it bothers you. But, if you cannot change it, learn to live with it. Be flexible. Give in once in a while. If you do, others are more likely to do so as well.

9. Put yourself in an environment (work, home, leisure) that fits with your needs and desires. If you hate desk jobs, don't accept a job that requires that you sit at a desk all day. If you hate to talk politics, don't hang out exclusively with people who love to talk politics, etc.

10. If you're finding that taking direct action is challenging for you, then ask someone for help and coaching. Others have likely been in similar situations and may have some tips to share with you.

BUILDING STRESS RESILIENCE

Social Support

11. Don't keep all your worries to yourself. Discussing your problems with a trusted friend can help clear your mind of confusion so you can concentrate on problem solving. Be willing to ask for help. It's not a sign of weakness. Rather, it's a sign that you're human and that you value others' input and insights. A burden shared is a burden reduced.

12. Don't do everything alone! Avoid isolating yourself and dodging people. Develop or renew relationships with friends and loved ones. Not only does closeness bring new insights, but it also helps soothe anxiety and depression.

13. Stop over-nurturing. People don't learn to solve their own issues or handle their responsibilities if you're routinely taking them on. Instead, learn to gracefully disengage when you need to do so.

BUILDING STRESS RESILIENCE

14. Develop friendships with non-worriers and complainers. Nothing can get you into the habit of worrying faster and complaining constantly than spending time with chronic worrywarts and complainers. If you must interact with them, learn to put boundaries around how much time you spend with them.

15. Form at least one or two high quality relationships with people you trust and can be yourself with. Associate mostly with peaceful and supportive people.

16. Work on strengthening your existing relationships. Create a list of the most important people in your life (work, play, family, etc.). Then identify: (a) how you can be more supportive of each person; and (b) how each person can support you. Think about a favor that you can do for others and do it. A little altruism never hurts, and it will make you feel better about yourself.

BUILDING STRESS RESILIENCE

Personal Care

17. Be aware of the unique combination of physical, mental, and emotional signals that your body sends when you're feeling stressed. Identify what triggers particular signals and find ways to address issues before your symptoms grow. Start small with one or two easy changes and work your way to bigger changes.

18. Food: Don't skip meals or abuse yourself with rigid unbalanced diets. Take care of yourself nutritionally by forming and keeping sensible eating habits. Focus on foods you like that are good for you. Minimize junk food. Eat sweets and salty snacks only rarely. Avoid or restrict how much caffeine you consume. Don't forget to take a lunch break. Try to get away from your desk or work area in body and mind, even if it's just for 15 or 20 minutes.

BUILDING STRESS RESILIENCE

19. Sleep: Don't disregard your need for sleep. Lack of sleep and rest will only make matters worse. Give your body a chance to recover from day to day. Go to sleep at about the same time every day. Get enough sleep, ensuring that you are sleeping for approximately 8 hours per day as needed. If necessary, set an alarm to remind yourself to go to bed.

20. Exercise: Physical outlets for stress help your body to fight off many of the negative effects of stress. Get up and stretch at least every half hour if your job requires that you sit for extended periods. Build in an exercise component to your lunch break. Combine strength training at least twice a week with at least 150 minutes of aerobic exercise per week to build your health to a high level of conditioning.

BUILDING STRESS RESILIENCE

21. Relaxation: Learn and practice the skill of deep relaxation and meditation. Do a Google search for "deep relaxation," "guided visualization," or "meditation," sample the many YouTube videos on these topics, and find your favorite.

22. If you need quiet time in a noisy environment, pop in some earplugs.

23. Check your breathing throughout the day, and before, during, and after high-pressure situations. When feeling stressed, most people tend to take short, shallow breaths. When you breathe like this, stale air isn't expelled, tissue oxidation is incomplete, and muscle tension frequently results. If you find that your stomach muscles are knotted and your breathing is shallow, try to relax all your muscles and take several deep, slow breaths. You might try the following yoga technique whenever you feel the need to relax. Inhale deeply through your nose for a count of eight.

BUILDING STRESS RESILIENCE

Hold your breath for a count of 10. Then, with lips puckered, exhale very slowly through your mouth for a count of 16, or for as long as you can. Concentrate on the long sighing sound, and feel the tension dissolve. Repeat 10 times.

24. Allow yourself time for privacy, quiet, and introspection. Find some time every day – even if only 10 minutes – for complete privacy, aloneness with your thoughts, and freedom from the pressures of work. Maintain personal rituals and comfortable patterns that help you rebound from stress.

25. If you smoke, stop completely. Minimize consumption of alcohol and eliminate the use of recreational drugs. Avoid binge drinking, which is consuming 5 or more alcoholic drinks for men and 4 or more alcoholic drinks for women within a 2 hour period. Nicotine, alcohol, and drugs may feel good in the moment, but they add to

your body's physical stresses, which makes dealing with external stresses much harder. Have an annual physical examination to provide extra peace of mind.

Control – Attitudes and Emotions

26. Diminish worry. Try to keep worrying to a minimum. It changes nothing. You'll have a better grip on your situation if you spend less time worrying and more time taking care of your needs.

27. Develop a sense of humor. Try to bring joy and happy moments into your life. It's hard to suffer from burnout when you're having fun and enjoying yourself.

28. Be aware of times when you're most likely to make rash decisions or say something inappropriate that you regret later. This may happen when you're hungry, lonely, stressed, feeling "cornered," or tired. In these cases, take a time out or say that

you'll think about or reflect on the matter before offering your opinion or decision.

29. Adopt a forgiving view of events and people. Accept the fact that we live in an imperfect world surrounded by imperfect people (yourself included).

30. Embrace an optimistic view of the world. Believe that most people are doing the best they can (yourself included).

31. "Worry about the pennies and the dollars will take care of themselves." That's another way of saying: take care of the todays as best you can, and the yesterdays and the tomorrows will take care of themselves. Live in the present moment, and do the best you can right now.

32. Become more flexible. Some things are worth getting done even if they're done imperfectly, and some issues are okay to compromise on.

BUILDING STRESS RESILIENCE

33. Eliminate destructive self-talk: "I'm not good enough...," "He'll never change...," "It's always stressful...," etc. It distorts our perceptions of situations and ourselves.

34. Do nothing which, after being done, leads you to tell a lie.

35. Write your thoughts and feelings in a journal (or on a sheet of paper to be thrown away). This can help you clarify your thoughts and transform your perspective of situations.

36. Inoculate yourself against a feared event. For example, before speaking in public, take time to go over every part of the experience in your mind. Imagine what you'll wear, what the audience will look like, how you will present your talk, what the questions will be and how you will answer them, etc. Visualize the experience the way you want it to it be. When you have to make the actual presentation, it

will feel familiar, and your anxiety will be lower.

Organizing Yourself

37. Schedule a realistic day aiming to accomplish two or three important tasks. Avoid the tendency to schedule back-to-back appointments. Instead, allow time between them for a breathing spell. Better yet, schedule thinking time and time to complete your important tasks.

38. Use your weekend time for a change of pace. If your work week is slow and structured, build in action and time for spontaneity into your weekends. If your work week is fast-paced and full of people and deadlines, seek peace and solitude during your days off.

39. Do one thing at a time. When you're busy with a project, concentrate on doing that project. Don't be distracted by other tasks.

BUILDING STRESS RESILIENCE

When you're with someone, be with that person and with no one and nothing else (yes, that includes your cell phone).

40. If you have an especially unpleasant task to do, get it done early in the day. Once you get it over with, the rest of your day will be free of anxiety.

41. Procrastination is stressful. Whatever you want to do tomorrow, do today; whatever you want to do today, do it now.

Personal Habits

42. Get up 15 minutes earlier in the morning. The inevitable morning mishaps will be less stressful. Prepare for the morning the evening before. Set the breakfast table, make lunches, put out the clothes you plan to wear, etc. Allow 15 minutes of extra time to get to appointments. Rushing = stress!

BUILDING STRESS RESILIENCE

43. Don't rely on your memory. Write down appointments, when to pick up the dry cleaning, when library books are due, etc.

44. Make duplicates of all keys and keep them in a safe place. Consider giving a house key to a trusted friend or neighbor.

45. Practice preventive maintenance. Your car, appliances, home, and relationships will be less likely to break down or fall apart at the worst possible moment. Plan ahead. Don't let the gas tank get below one-quarter full; keep a well-stocked "emergency shelf" of home staples; don't wait until you're down to your last bus token or postage stamp to buy more; etc.

46. Don't put up with something that doesn't work properly. If your wallet, shoelaces, windshield wipers – whatever – are a constant irritation, get them fixed, or get new ones.

BUILDING STRESS RESILIENCE

47. Create order out of chaos. Organize your home and workspace so that you always know exactly where things are. Have a place for everything, and put things where they belong right away so you don't go through the stress of losing things.

48. Use your waiting time (grocery store line-up, doctor's office, etc.) effectively.

49. Set up contingency plans, just in case (e.g. "If for some reason either of us is delayed, here's what we'll do..." or "If we get split up in the shopping center, here's where we'll meet."). Ask questions. Taking a few moments to repeat directions, what someone expects of you, etc., can save hours. (This is the old "the *hurrieder* I go, the *behinder* I get" idea.)

50. Learn to pace yourself. Try to take life in moderation. You only have so much energy available. Figure out what you want and need in your life, and balance work

with love, pleasure, and relaxation. Manage your life as you would manage an important organization. Don't become lopsided in any one area; seek rewarding experiences in all dimensions of life (social, physical, emotional, spiritual). Don't let your work dominate your life. Do you work to live…or live to work?

51. Be open to new experiences. Find self-renewing opportunities. Try doing things that you've never done before, sample foods that you've never eaten, and go places that you've never been. Read interesting books and articles to freshen your ideas and broaden your points of view. Solicit and listen to others' ideas and opinions in order to learn from them. Reduce or eliminate television watching, Internet surfing, and playing you're your cellphone. Have one or more pastimes that is relaxing and that doesn't involve having "something to show for it."

BUILDING STRESS RESILIENCE

Actions for Reducing Your Employees' Stress

1. Give employees the gift of trust and the freedom to make decisions about work. Delegate appropriately.

2. Give employees opportunities to participate in decisions and actions affecting their jobs. Include them, give them information, and help them feel like they belong to a team. Avoid isolation tactics such as: withholding information, not inviting them to meetings, shelving people, not noticing others' work or suggestions, or playing favorites.

3. Provide opportunities for social interaction among employees and "time to unwind."

4. Provide employees with time and space so that they don't feel that they have too much to do all at once, all the time.

BUILDING STRESS RESILIENCE

5. Improve communications with employees. Listen to their words, feelings, and needs.

6. Give employees appreciation for doing good work. Share credit for successes at work.

7. Reduce employees' uncertainty about career development and future employment prospects. Provide a clear picture of what you expect of them.

8. Redistribute workloads wisely. Ensure that they fit with employees' capabilities and resources. Design jobs to provide meaning, stimulation, and opportunities for employees to use their skills. Establish flexible work schedules that are compatible with demands and responsibilities outside the job.

9. Manage your own stress. Research clearly demonstrates that managerial stress is contagious. If you're stressed, then your

employees will be stressed. In part, this may be due to the fact that they are working in the same environment as you, which may itself be the source of stress. However, managers need to serve as role models for their employees in many ways, including how they handle stress.

Now that you have read these tips, review the ones that you have circled, checked, or highlighted. What do they have in common?

4

DILEMMAS: WHAT WOULD YOU DO?

Now you have the opportunity to consider how to apply what you just learned in a sampling of situations. For each dilemma, read the situation, and answer the reflection questions presented at the end of each situation.

BUILDING STRESS RESILIENCE

Bob too Busy to Delegate

Bob decided to hire an assistant because he knew he needed help. He hoped that the assistant would "see" what needed to be done and simply jump right in and start doing it. However, because Bob was too busy to tell his assistant Pat what needed to be done, Pat was confused and anxious. To top it off, Bob felt that all tasks and decisions – however small – needed to be vetted by him. This created a major bottleneck, since he was fairly disorganized and often found on his phone or darting in and out of meetings.

Pat tried to figure out what needed to be done on his own since his attempts to meet with Bob were unsuccessful (he would sit in Bob's office when they were supposed to meet, but Bob would simply talk on the phone or shoo him away). One day, Pat created a to-do list, hoping to define some responsibilities and tasks for himself. He emailed it to Bob including a line that said that, if he hadn't heard from Bob in 3 days, he would presume that Bob agreed with the to-do list. Naturally, Bob didn't respond within 3 days, so Pat started to carry out the responsibilities he had identified for himself, one of which was to organize paperwork and files on Bob's desk.

When Bob returned to his office after a lengthy meeting, he flew into a rage when he saw that his desk was neatly organized. He felt that his "private space" had been violated and that he could no longer find anything. He quickly ushered Pat out his office and told him to make himself useful – somewhere else.

Who is feeling stressed in this situation?
What could Bob and Pat have done differently?
If you were Bob's management coach, what would you say to him?

BUILDING STRESS RESILIENCE

Janet Jaded by her Job

Although Janet used to wake up in the morning excited by the challenges of her upcoming work day, she now pressed her snooze button several times and dragged herself out of bed and, eventually, into work. Her work life felt flat, stale, and routine. She did what was expected – but not much more. She was able to hide her fading energy level by minimizing her interactions with her colleagues and simply exchanging sarcastic or cynical comments about work with them.

When Janet joined the organization a few years ago, she was eager to make a contribution. She had joined this organization after several stints at other companies that, unlike this one, had no pension plans or benefits. This was to be her final employer for the final 15 years of her career.

The joy Janet took in building relationships with clients and helping them discover new solutions became muted over time. She became a "by the book" person,

BUILDING STRESS RESILIENCE

never looking for new opportunities. Janet became afraid to "be herself" on the job: instead of being friendly, she was "all business." Over time, Janet realized that her ideas and suggestions for improvement were not welcomed. She was told that there was no budget available and that she should simply focus on doing her job as best she can with the resources she has available to her.

At the end of the work day, Janet went home, made herself a big bowl of pasta and ate it while downing a six-pack of beer and watching TV. Sometimes, she indulged in brownies. She would decline offers to go out because she felt down in the dumps.

What are the causes of Janet's stress?
If you were Janet, what would you do?
If you were Janet's manager, what would you say to her?

BUILDING STRESS RESILIENCE

Patricia Feeling Pressure to Perform

When Patricia received her PhD, she assumed that the rest of her life as a professor would be smooth sailing. However, her first job as an assistant professor offered Patricia a reality check. Patricia was scared that she couldn't keep up with the work demands.

She was expected to teach three different classes per semester. The classes and class times were chosen by the program manager. In preparing for her classes, Patricia remembered that she was expected to be a dynamic, inspiring professor, maintain high standards of rigor, give students extensive and immediate feedback on their exams and assignments, and receive very high teaching evaluations from her students.

If that wasn't enough, Patricia needed to have an active research and publication program, ensuring that she applied for (and received) research grants regularly and published at least five articles in high quality publications within five years. Each grant application required about 100 hours of work, and each publication required more than 1000 hours of concentrated work, depending on data gathering requirements and the number of revisions required and rejections received.

Finally, Patricia was expected to participate in a variety of faculty committees, taking an average of eight hours per week. This combined with her other responsibilities and the need to be visible and highly collegial left Patricia scrambling and unsure how to meet the extensive prerequisites for obtaining tenure in five years. One of her colleagues was eating her meals in her office and regularly sleeping overnight at work. Patricia didn't want to resort to working into the wee hours of the night. She was already putting in 10 to 12 hour days and sneaking into her home office after her husband and children were asleep.

What are the causes of Patricia's stress?
If you were Patricia, what would you do?

BUILDING STRESS RESILIENCE

Darwin Drowning in Work

Every single day of the week, when Darwin finishes his work day, there are still piles of work left undone. Any plans he makes for the day are disrupted by constant emergencies and other tasks that take his attention away from the significant parts of his job. And his boss simply tells him to do the best he can (with no increase in budget, of course).

As a competent and experienced I.T. guy, Darwin is called to deal with emergencies caused by failing equipment, power outages, client errors and issues, and blunders made by contractors and other employees. Typically, on evenings and weekends, he receives a dozen emails signaling issues that he needs to address the next day. He also fills in for three other colleagues while they're away due to vacations or illness (a weekly occurrence). An easygoing guy who wants to be a team player, Darwin has trouble saying "no" to requests for his help.

BUILDING STRESS RESILIENCE

Days, weeks, and months pass by, and Darwin has nothing but hundreds of 'emergencies' to show for his use of time. He feels helpless to make any changes; "This is just the way my job is," he consoles himself. So, he simply carries on as best he can, being sure to take his coffee and lunch breaks and leave work exactly at 5 pm. He doesn't bring any work home with him, but when lying in bed at night, Darwin thinks about the day's problems. His wife notices that he's frowning and tossing and turning.

What are the causes of Darwin's stress?
If you were Darwin, what would you do?

5

PLANNING FOR ACTION

Answer the following questions in your learning journal.

1. What are my top three stressors?
2. How would I categorize my current approach to dealing with each stressor (flight, fight, or flow)?
3. Is what I'm thinking and doing helping me deal with my stress?

BUILDING STRESS RESILIENCE

4. What is working well for me?
5. What isn't working for me?
6. What is it about these stressors that is causing stress for me?
7. Can I eliminate the stressors altogether? (If so, how?)
8. What can I control about the stressors?
   a. How can I think differently?
   b. How can I feel differently?
   c. How can I take care of my body?
   d. What else can I do differently (e.g., engage in problem solving, communicate directly with the people involved, seek support, organize and manage my space and use of time)?
9. Is it possible and does it make more sense to avoid the stressors (e.g., walk away; let go; say "no"; delegate; withdraw; know your limits)? If so, what will you do?
10. If it is not possible (or advisable) to either address or avoid the stressors, is it possible to live with them or "accept" them (e.g., equip yourself for coping with them; build your resistance spiritually; socially,

physically, or mentally; change your perceptions about yourself, others, or the situation)?
11. Starting now, what five specific actions will you take to manage your stress effectively?

About the Managerial Competencies Series

What's in the series?

This series is built around four managerial competency clusters: personal, people, purpose, and process.

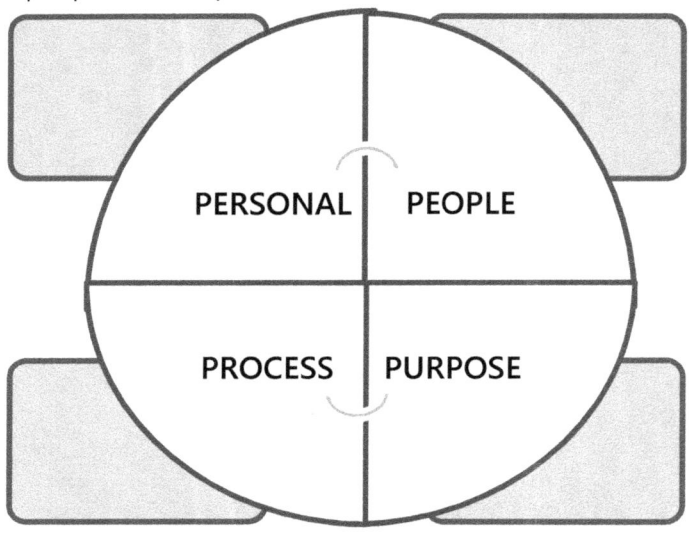

BUILDING STRESS RESILIENCE

Each cluster is made up of several competencies possessed by awesome managers. The series addresses a total of 15 competencies, each of which is the topic of a book of around 100 pages. Let's look at each cluster one at a time.

Personal Competencies

The starting point of the series is developing personal skills, given that effective self-management is essential for managing people, programs, and processes. It goes without saying that to manage others, you first must be able to manage yourself. People who are familiar with their personal strengths and challenges and who engage in effective self-management tend to work well with others.

BUILDING STRESS RESILIENCE

Here are the competencies included in the Personal Competencies cluster:

1. **Living the Core Values**, which involves demonstrating honesty, truthfulness, trustworthiness, reliability, fairness, and ethicality in all your decisions and interactions.
2. **Developing Personal Mastery** through personal responsibility, emotional resilience, constructive attitudes, self-confidence, adaptability, conscientiousness, and competence.
3. **Organizing Yourself** by focusing on your priorities and making effective use of time.

BUILDING STRESS RESILIENCE

4. **Building Stress Resilience**, which deals with managing life's stresses by developing personal hardiness.

People Competencies

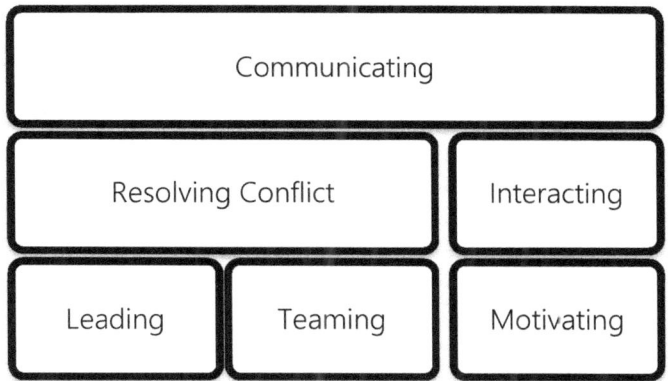

This cluster helps you examine and build your skills in working with and managing others. Although it's important for managers to be *technically* competent in order to gain credibility, interpersonal skills make the difference between awesome and not-so-awesome managers.

BUILDING STRESS RESILIENCE

The competencies included in the People Competencies cluster are:

5. **Communicating in Writing and through Presentations**, which focuses on communicating ideas effectively, whether verbally or in writing.
6. **Creating Engagement**, creating motivating working conditions so that staff contribute their best to the organization.
7. **Building Relationships**, which considers how to interact with others through effective listening and responding.
8. **Resolving Conflict**, which addresses how to deal with conflict in a productive manner.
9. **Leading Your Team**, which means leading in a manner that is appropriate for the needs of the situation and your team.
10. **Cultivating Team Spirit** by building a cohesive, high-performing team.

BUILDING STRESS RESILIENCE

Purpose and Process Competencies

This final cluster combines two sets of competencies. Purpose competencies offer you a "big picture" perspective of your organization and your own role in the organization. Process competencies help you translate this "big picture" (the *whats*) into everyday practice (the *hows*). In other words, they allow you to consider how work should be done as a means of accomplishing the goals of your organization and your work unit.

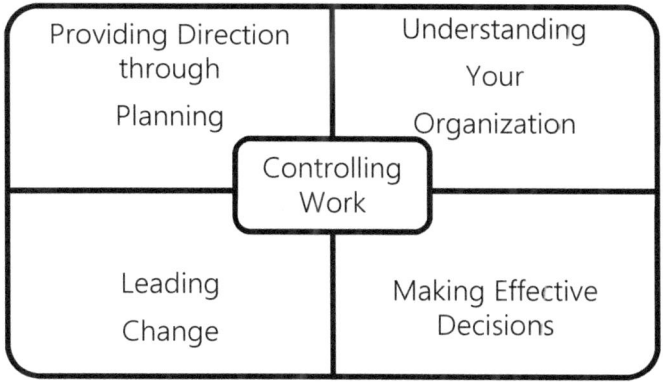

BUILDING STRESS RESILIENCE

Purpose and Process competencies include:

11. **Making Effective Decisions**, whether individually or in a team setting.
12. **Controlling Work Performance** by establishing control mechanisms to ensure results.
13. **Providing Direction through Planning**, which discusses the management process and offers tips for setting organizational direction and developing operational plans that fit this direction.
14. **Understanding Your Organization**, in other words, understanding the principles of organizing work and creating the right structure for your work unit.
15. **Leading Change** so that your organization and team thrive.

How is each book organized?

Each book is organized according to a five-step learning process. This process is designed to help you learn in an active and reflective manner.

In each book, after a brief introduction, we jump right into the "**reality check**." This series of self-coaching questions is meant to help you reflect on and develop insight into your own strengths and weaknesses in relation to a particular competence and, hopefully, motivate you to work on building your competencies.

BUILDING STRESS RESILIENCE

The reality check consists of the kinds of questions that management coaches might ask you, but that you can simply ask yourself. Just be sure to give yourself a chance to answer them!

Management coaches help managers view and understand situations from a variety of perspectives. But, if the art of coaching is asking challenging questions (as management coach Chantal Binet says), why not ask yourself these questions?

Second, to accompany you on your learning journey, you're offered a curated collection of **inspirational quotes**. There's lots of wisdom available from people from all walks of life. The quotes that grab us and speak to us do so because they have touched a nerve in us. They resonate with us, perhaps because they offer a message that we need to hear to continue developing or because they challenge us to become better people.

Third, we offer you tons of **tips and tricks** of awesome managers. These practical tips cover a gamut of perspectives and actions that you can take to improve your competencies. Ideally, they will encourage you to consider the variety of possibilities and alternatives that are available to you. It's up to you to decide which are the most useful to you. As you read this section, be sure to note or highlight the tips that stand out for you.

Next, we present a series of **dilemmas** or situations for you to resolve. This section will help you see how you might apply the tips and tricks from the previous section. We ask you to read the situation and then identify what you would do in these situations. You might choose one of the alternatives that is offered, or you might come up with your own creative solution. Ultimately, there are many factors and perspectives that might influence what is the "best" choice.

Finally, we nudge you to develop an **action plan** that you will *actually* implement. Developing and implementing an action plan is an especially important step because it helps you draw value from your efforts in working through this series. After all, you're reading this

BUILDING STRESS RESILIENCE

book because you're hoping to become an awesome manager, right? This means developing a realistic plan that describes the actions that you intend to take to become an awesome manager, implementing your plan, reflecting on how well it worked, and then continuously making any adjustments that are needed. So, the cycle starts again!

How can you get the most out of the series?

You can read one or two books per month for an entire year, creating and implementing action plans for each book. Ultimately, this will help you develop a better understanding of yourself as a manager, your expectations, your strengths, and your areas for improvement.

As a way of refreshing your competencies, you can even re-read the books and re-visit your action plans in the future. Depending on what's happening in your life (new job, new team, new challenges), every time you read these books, you may develop new insights that help you deal with a situation.

BUILDING STRESS RESILIENCE

> The knowledge of the world is only to be acquired in the world, and not in a closet.
> *Lord Chesterfield*

> What we have to learn to do,
> we learn by doing.
> *Aristotle*

> Life is a succession of lessons which must be lived to be understood.
> *Ralph Waldo Emerson*

What do this British statesman from the 1600s, Greek philosopher from 384 B.C., and American poet from the 1800s have in common? They all agree that learning comes from trying new things, not from simply sitting back and reading a book.

Don't just read the books; *do* them! Just reading the books won't transform you into an awesome manager. If you just read the books, you might get to know a lot about what it means to be an awesome manager without changing what you do in the workplace. How useful is that? Just like learning to ride a bike, it's impossible to develop your skills by simply reading or even thinking about what you have read. Besides, as *The Matrix* reminds us, "There's a difference between knowing the path and walking it."

In order to truly learn from our experiences, we need to do a complete loop of the learning cycle: we need to reflect on our experiences, figure out what lessons we learned, consider ways to apply these lessons, and then apply them. You may know people who seem to repeat the same mistakes over and over again or people who continually approach situations in a manner that doesn't work for them. It's probably because they go through life without taking the time to reflect, consider what they've learned, and develop an action plan in order to change their experiences. They're stuck somewhere on the learning cycle. David Kolb, the creator of this learning cycle, says that we all have a favorite place on the cycle where we tend to get stuck.

BUILDING STRESS RESILIENCE

Some people simply enjoy reading the books and reflecting on how they may relate to their lives, hopefully finding an opportunity to make use of their learning at some point in the future. However, without specific goals and action plans, they're not extracting as much value as they could from their investment of time and money.

Although this is partly due to differences in learning styles, it's also due to a reluctance to try something new and different. This may be caused by a fear of stepping out of one's comfort zone: what is familiar is comfortable. It may also be caused by a desire to accumulate a truckload of knowledge or have the perfect circumstances, such as the ideal boss or set of employees, before acting. Some of us think and think and continue to think without taking action. That used to be my personal downfall until I realized that knowing lots about a topic isn't the same as learning or making a difference in real life!

At the other extreme, some of us take action without first reflecting on our experiences and what we learned from them. Some people prefer to go ahead and try things out right away. They're more action-oriented than their reflective counterparts. These folks typically find it especially challenging to slow down, consciously reflect on what they're reading, and develop a well thought out action plan before acting. In the same way, if you just read the books and do nothing else, the learning process will get stuck right off the bat.

Reflecting and taking action is the best solution. It's not enough to *know* how to do something. Although it's helpful and important to take the time to reflect and develop insights, at some point, you need to *do* the work yourself. Otherwise, as management expert Peter Block has said, "Waiting becomes an excuse for not acting."

Here are **five other important things** to do to maximize your learning. First, **keep a learning journal**. Record your thoughts as you read the books, answer the self-coaching questions, and develop your action plans. It will help you clarify your thinking, see patterns in what you have been experiencing and writing, and serve as a record of commitments you have made to yourself through your action plans. You'll be able to look back at what you've written and be impressed with all that you've learned! You could use a notebook or create an electronic document. Some people even email journal entries to themselves as a way of recording the day and time of their entries.

Second, **pull together a feedback team** who can help you get the most from this series. Your feedback team could be a group of four or five people that you have confidence in, such as coworkers, your manager, friends, and family members. Don't be shy about asking people for their support in helping you become a better manager; they are more willing to help you than you might think! These discussions will offer you different perspectives and exponentially increase how much you learn from the series. Besides, awesome managers surround themselves with people they trust who are willing to give them honest feedback that will help them grow as individuals.

In supporting you, others can play one or more of the following roles:

→ The Head: These people can help you analyze a question or problem objectively. They can sketch out options, compare data, or simply provide you with accurate information.
→ The Heart: These people can help you express your emotions and understand them better. They listen, cheer you up, don't make judgments, and give you a sense of security.
→ The Legs/Arms: These people help you do things. They go places with you; they make you get moving when you don't feel like it. These people energize you.

How can your manager help? Can your manager provide feedback, advice and tips, and time to complete the series? What will you do to get your manager's help? For example, could you meet with your manager once every two weeks to discuss your progress and talk about how to manage effectively?

How can your peers help? Can your peers provide feedback, tips about managing, or coaching when needed? What will you do to get their help? Could you schedule a coffee break with them once every two weeks to discuss what you're learning and to share tips? Can you work through the series together?

How can your employees help? Can your employees provide feedback regarding your strengths and opportunities for improvement or work with you to develop a plan for making your unit function more effectively? What will you do to get their help? Could you meet with them once every two weeks to discuss what you're learning and how your team can implement elements of your action plan?

How can your friends help? Could they provide feedback, tips about managing, and encouragement for you to try new things?

BUILDING STRESS RESILIENCE

What will you do to get their help? Could you organize a dinner with them once every two weeks to discuss what you're learning and how to implement your action plan?

Third, **develop and implement a SMARTER action plan.** You know you've really learned something when your behavior changes (for the better, of course).

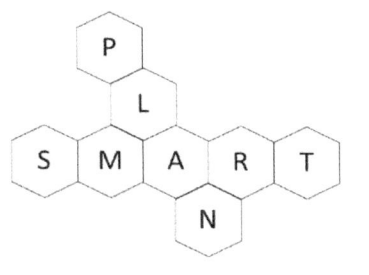

Insights and tips that are meaningful to you will change your perspective *and* your behaviors. That's why each book ends by inviting you to develop an action plan. Your plan should be **Specific, Measurable, Attainable, Realistic, Timely, Exciting, and Rewarded.** Think about things that you need to start doing, stop doing, or continue doing. Here's an example: "By the end of next week, I will write two letters – one to my former manager and one to my best friend – expressing my gratitude for their coaching and willingness to challenge me to become a better person. I will send these letters by email no later than Friday afternoon." Write your action plan in your journal. Revisit it to check your progress, and revise your plan as needed. Remember to ask for help from others, evaluate your progress, and reward yourself for your progress toward becoming an awesome manager.

Fourth, **identify obstacles or barriers that might get in your way of making the most of the series** and implementing your action plans; for example, lack of time or energy, poor personal habits, others' expectations, etc. List these in the column labelled "Obstacles" on the following page. Now, think about specific actions that you can take to address them and place these in the "Neutralizers" column; for example, meet with your manager, plan small wins or ways to celebrate your progress, etc.

BUILDING STRESS RESILIENCE

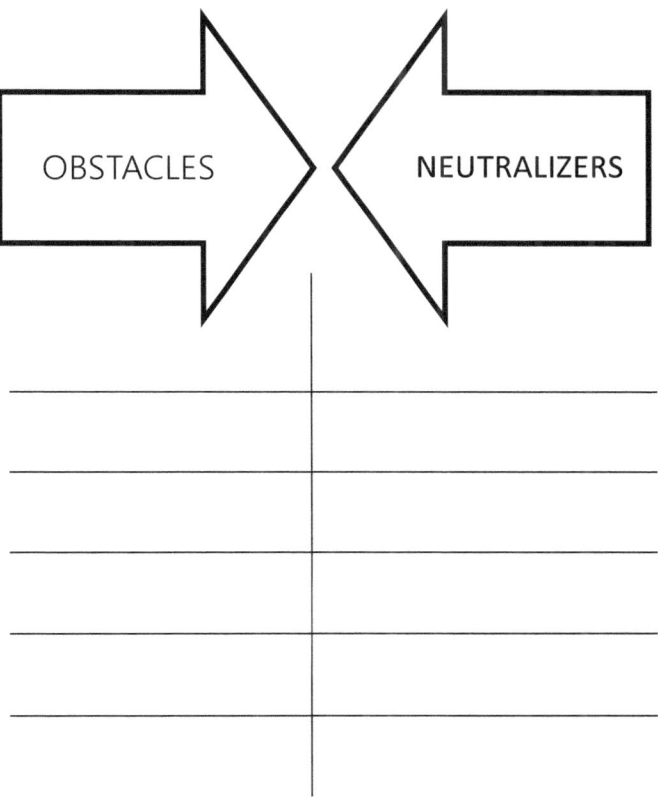

Finally, do what you need to do to motivate yourself. Don't wait to be motivated to get started. Instead, get started, and motivation will come knocking at your door!

BUILDING STRESS RESILIENCE

Also, try to be comfortable with discomfort. As you change how you manage, you may meet with some resistance from those around you. You exist in a system of relationships. Because systems are geared toward equilibrium (stability), if you change one thing in the system, the equilibrium is shot, and the system is upset. There may be pressure from others and from your own sense of comfort for you to do what you've always done regardless of whether or not it works.

It may be tempting to give up when things feel unnatural, but rest assured that this is part of the learning process. It's normal that trying out new ways of doing things makes you feel a bit uncomfortable in one way or another. Sometimes, we come across awesome folks who do their work without hesitation and seemingly without effort. It's easy to forget that they've gone through the highs and lows of the learning process. For example, think of Cirque du Soleil acrobats who seem to perform stunts with ease and pinpoint accuracy. It took them lots of practice, repetition, and even occasional failures to get to that skill level. Experts make things look easy.

Are you ready to begin your awesome journey? Earl Nightingale once said, "All you need is the plan, the road map, and the courage to press on to your destination." I hope that this series serves as your guide and road map on your journey toward awesomeness.

REFERENCES

American Lung Association. *52 Proven Stress Reducers.* http://www.freedomfromsmoking.org

Anschuetz, B. L. (1999). The high cost of caring: Coping with workplace stress. Sharing: Epilepsy Ontario. Cited by the Canadian Centre for Occupational Health and Safety at http://ccohs.ca/oshanswers/psychosocial/stress.html.

Cook, D. (2017). Workplace stress costing employers $500 billion annually. Retrieved from: www.benefitspro.com/2017/10/20/ workplace-stress-costing-employers-500-billion-ann/?slreturn=20180609174957

Davis, M. Eshelman, E. R., McKay, M. (2008). *The relaxation & stress reduction workbook.* Oakland, CA: New Harbinger Publications.

Freudenberger, H. J. (1975). The staff burn-out syndrome in alternative institutions. *Psychotherapy: Theory, Research & Practice*, 12 (1): 73 – 82.

Gordon, Arthur. (1959). A day at the beach. *Reader's Digest.*

Gugel, R. (2017) Tips and techniques for dealing with stress. *Today's Caregiver.* http://www.caregiver.com/articles/dealing-with-stress/

Nachen Gugel, R. (2017). Tips and Techniques for Dealing with Stress. Today's CareGiver. Retrieved from: https://caregiver.com/articles/dealing-with-stress/

New Zealand Health Services (no date) Mental health tips. Retrieved from: http://www.everybody.co.nz/features/mentalhealth.html

Seyle, H. (1946). The general adaptation syndrome and the diseases of adaptation. *Journal of Clinical Endocrinology*, 6 (2): 119 – 131.

Texas Women's University Counseling and Psychological Services (no date). Retrieved from +http://www.twu.edu/o-sl/counseling/SH01html

Tubesing & Tubesing; Davis, M. et al. (1988). *Structured Exercises in Stress Management*, Vol. 1, Whole Person Associates.

Please note: some of the web links may no longer be active at the time of publication.

BUILDING STRESS RESILIENCE

BUILDING STRESS RESILIENCE

Playbooks in the Managerial Competencies Series

1. Living the Core Values
2. Developing Personal Mastery
3. Organizing Yourself
4. Building Stress Resilience
5. Communicating in Writing and Through Presentations
6. Creating Engagement
7. Building Relationships
8. Resolving Conflict
9. Leading Your Team
10. Cultivating Team Spirit
11. Making Effective Decisions
12. Controlling Work Performance
13. Providing Direction through Planning
14. Understanding Your Organization
15. Leading Change

www.ingramcontent.com/pod-product-compliance
Lightning Source LLC
Chambersburg PA
CBHW070304230526
45470CB00002B/721